Centipedes

Rebecca Rissman

www.raintreepublishers.co.uk
Visit our website to find out more information about Raintree books.

To order:
☎ Phone 0845 6044371
🖨 Fax +44 (0) 1865 312263
✉ Email myorders@raintreepublishers.co.uk

Customers from outside the UK please telephone +44 1865 312262

Raintree is an imprint of Capstone Global Library Limited, a company incorporated in England and Wales having its registered office at 7 Pilgrim Street, London, EC4V 6LB – Registered company number: 6695582

Text © Capstone Global Library Limited 2013
First published in hardback in 2013
The moral rights of the proprietor have been asserted.

Edited by Dan Nunn, Rebecca Rissman, and Catherine Veitch
Designed by Joanna Hinton-Malivoire
Picture research by Mica Brancic
Originated by Capstone Global Library Ltd
Production by Victoria Fitzgerald
Printed in China by South China Printing Company Ltd

ISBN 978 1 406 24134 1
16 15 14 13 12
10 9 8 7 6 5 4 3 2 1

British Library Cataloguing in Publication Data
Rissman, Rebecca.
Centipedes. – (Creepy crawlies)
595.6'2-dc22
A full catalogue record for this book is available from the British Library.

Acknowledgements
We would like to thank the following for permission to reproduce photographs: Alamy pp. 15 (© ephotocorp/Vivek Gour-Broome), 16 (© NaturePics); Corbis p. 14 (© Alex Wild/Visuals Unlimited); Dreamstime pp. 5 (© Bruce MacQueen), 23 (© Aetmeister, © Alexey Romanov); Dreamstime.com p. 23 (© Dreamam); Getty Images p. 12 (National Geographic/George Grall); iStockphoto pp. 7 (© Emmanouil Filippou), 19 (© Laurie Knight), 22 (© Emmanouil Filippou), 23 (© arlindo71); Shutterstock pp. 1 & 11 (© tomatito), 8 (© Anton Chernenko), 10 (© Pan Xunbin), 13 (© ex0rzist), 17 (© Menno Schaefer), 21 (© Elliotte Rusty Harold), 22 (© Alex Staroseltsev, fivespots, Irin-k, © Photolinc).

Cover photograph of a centipede, reproduced with permission of Getty Images (Gallo Images/Danita Delimont).

Every effort has been made to contact copyright holders of any material reproduced in this book. Any omissions will be rectified in subsequent printings if notice is given to the publisher.

The publishers would like to thank Michael Bright for his assistance in the preparation of this book.

2

Contents

Let's search!

Legs, legs, and even more legs!
Which bug can you see?

A long, thin body with legs galore?
A centipede it must be!

5

The centipede's **long** body is covered in a hard, strong case.

It keeps the centipede protected as it moves from place to place.

6

7

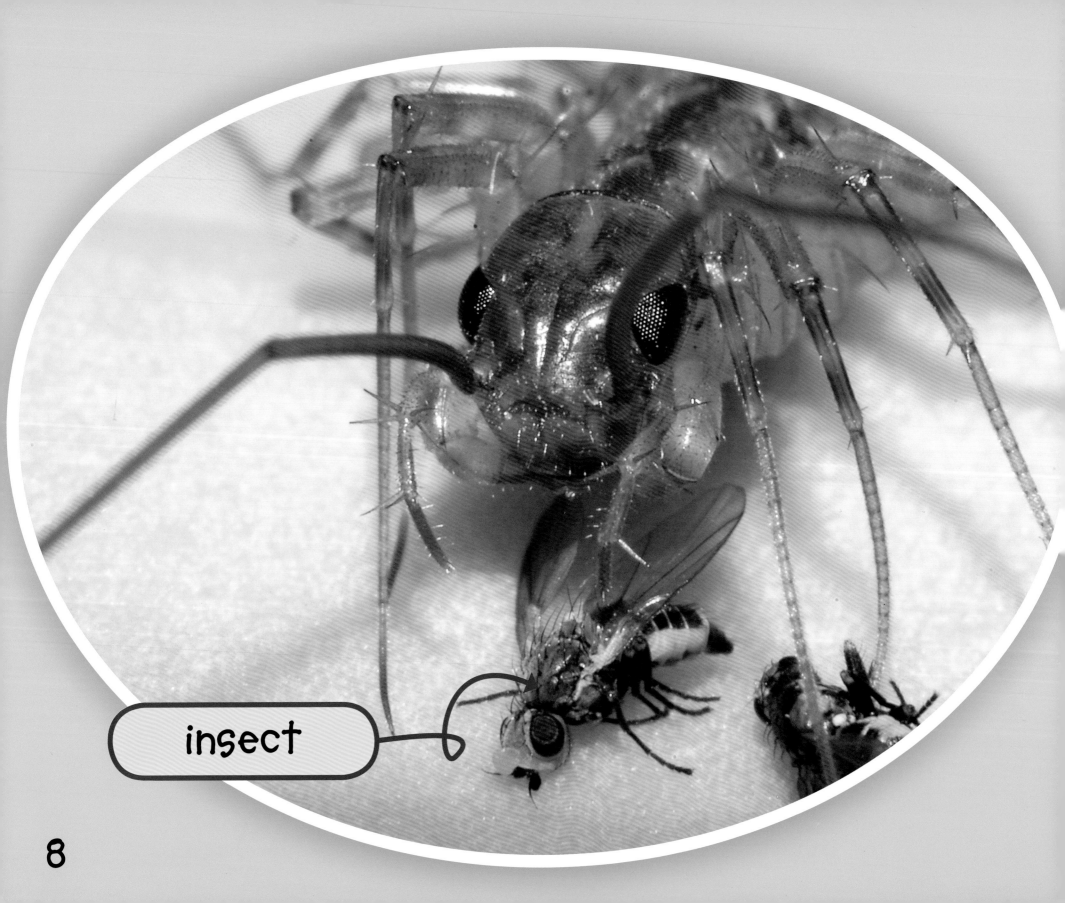

insect

Mouthparts help a centipede eat its food. It chomps until it's done.

So tell all the tiny insects,
if they get too close, to run!

Can you see the centipede's antennae?
They stick out from its head.

antennae

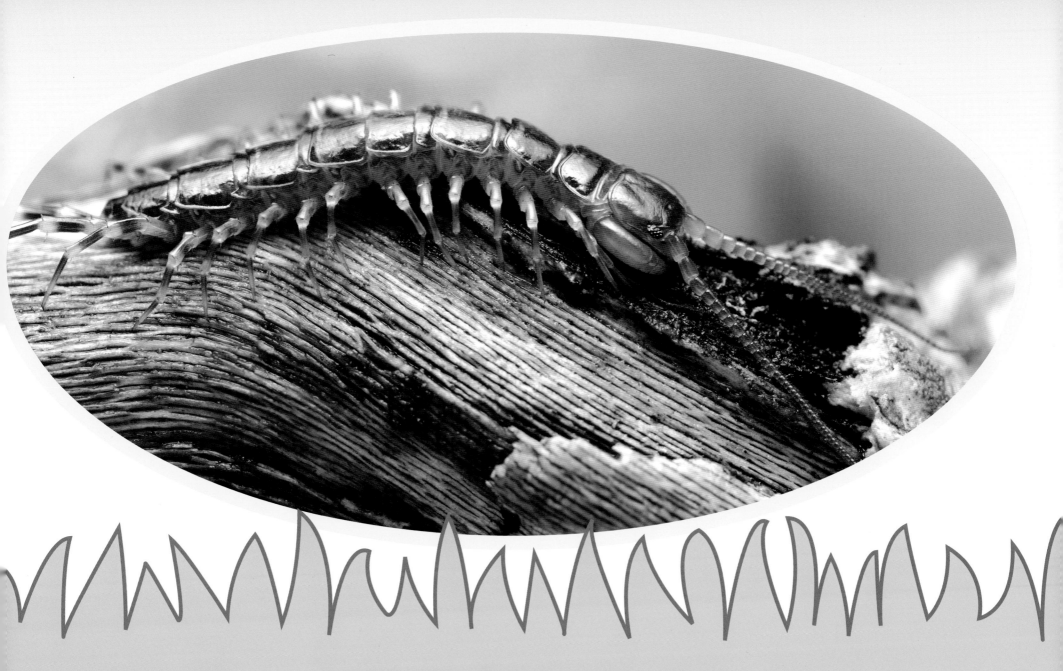

They help it find its way around
by feeling the ground ahead.

Some centipedes are brown or red.
Some centipedes are black.

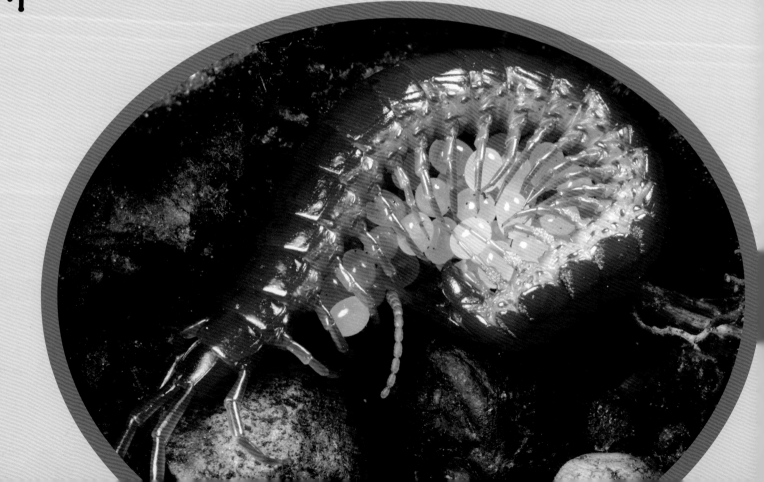

Some centipede colours help them hide,
so enemies won't attack.

Centipedes lay many eggs, which can be yellow, brown, or white.

Some centipedes guard their eggs by curling their bodies up tight.

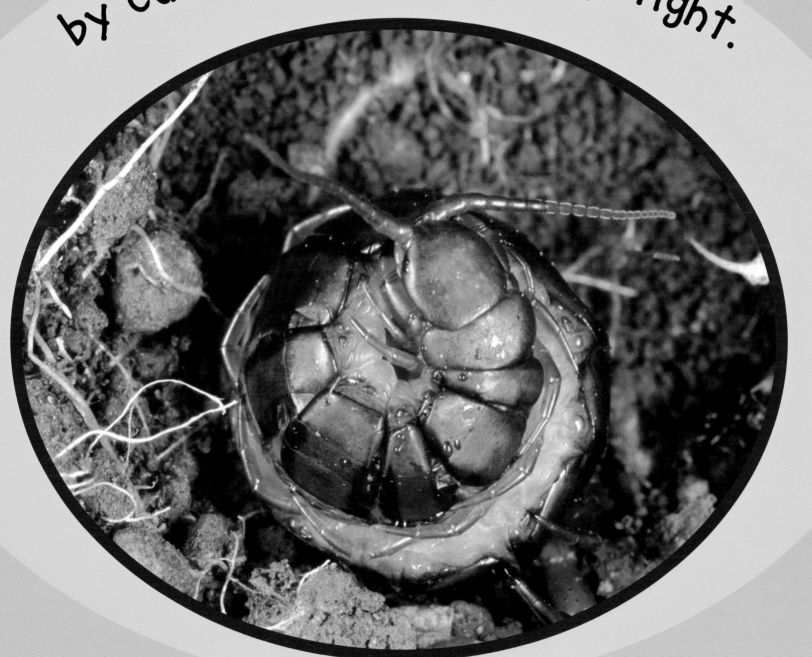

Most centipedes eat other bugs, which may not seem that nice!

Big centipedes eat birds and spiders. Some even eat mice!

Some centipedes use
their fangs to pinch or bite.

They scare away an enemy
if it tries to start a fight.

fang

Where can you find centipedes?
Try searching in dark, tight spaces.

Centipedes live under leaves and
rocks, and in other shadowy places.

Counting centipedes

How many centipedes can you count here?

Look high and low, and the answer will be clear!

23

Did you know?

Some centipedes glow in the dark! Have you seen one?

Index

24